P9-EAN-931

One Part Love

One Part Love

by

Babette Deutsch

New York
Oxford University Press
1939

DISCARDED

COPYRIGHT, 1939, BY OXFORD UNIVERSITY PRESS, NEW YORK, INC.

FIRST EDITION

PRINTED IN THE UNITED STATES OF AMERICA

For
AVRAHM

. . . We are one part love
And nine parts bitter thought.

John Crowe Ransom.

Acknowledgments

Certain of these poems have been published in *The Atlantic Monthly*, *Harpers' Magazine*, *The Nation*, *The New Republic*, *The New Yorker*, *Poetry*, *The Saturday Review of Literature*, *The Virginia Quarterly*, *The Yale Review*, and other periodicals.

Contents

I

II

III

I

Escape Denied

From sullen streets, from windows dismally smiling,
From the tall avenues that alchemize
A desperate luxury: on plates of gold
Offering silver fruits, as though the sun
Held lesser moons to eat. From the known seasons:
The sticky buds, the dusty leaves, the rains,
From snows that taste of childhood on the tongue
And so dissolve, betraying memory.
From various rooms: the wide one with the tables
Screens and couches for the wine-lit night,
As from the shabbiest in which time is folded
In the same creases morning after morning,
Where shall we find deliverance?
                                        An island,
That has no streets, no rooms,
And but one season.
Gifted with the sea's changes, kindled
By the horizon's legendary promise.

The exile on that coast who lies at ease
Breathing the island airs,
Knows where he lies.
In no far hour
Endures the cries of shipwreck, may yet see
The clutching hands hacked at the bloody wrist,
The raft
Sink with its selfish cargo.
Later feels
The shore shudder under enemy planes,
Faces, unarmed,

15

DISCARDED

72956

Invasion from above.
                    Heart, we have need of islands.
We have need of scenes
Whose pure felicity is slashed with rival
Colors that all become it.
And winds blowing
Sweet, then salt.
Though it be
Short as a soldier's furlough, hemmed with war,
There we shall mend our wounds,
We shall be well,
Bathing the past in strangeness, each day making
New memories, bright *décors* for the home
That we shall build if ever peace is signed
If we are still alive.

Confined within the hypocritic dream,
Measure its boundaries,
But receive its bounty
With grateful lips.
Knowing deliverance is brief, knowing
The war goes on after it is declared,
No victory final,
No island safe.
Look on this beauty with remorseless joy,
Knowing escape denied.

Afternoon Concert

The music rises like a waft of honey
As from cut flowers;
In parquet chairs lean, earnestly at ease,
The solid citizens who feel their money
Well spent on hours like these.

The pure cry of the violins, despairing,
On treads of air
Climbs, while with stifled hearts and ruffled scores,
They also climb who only sit here staring
At joy's abandoned shores.

The shrewder will be safe, the concert over,
When they will go
Back to the streets, the rooms they lately crossed
And once possessed. At home they shall recover
What on these heights was lost.

The slender cry is stilled, the monster sorrow
Remains. But not for these,
Who wholly self-possessed now slowly move
Toward the wide doors, the usual tomorrow,
Where all's to spend but love.

Words for a Lullaby

The thug is on the staircase,
The spy is on the roof,
And God lies in a cellar
For that is bullet-proof;
While kings play *opéra bouffe*.

The wars are not soon over
That tear the world apart,
And pile with dreadful droppings
Both shattered wall and heart,
To give fresh fires a start.

In vain to look for refuge.
Is it in vain to fight?
A few are born to courage,
And few to earn delight,
Struggling to meet the night.

Yet children craving stories
Must hear before they sleep
Wonders enough to dream on,
Though men may want to weep.
Those tears will keep.

Lines Written in Time of Peace

What shall we do with country quiet now?
A motor drones insanely in the blue
Like a bad bird in a dream.
Fear nothing. Hush.
The giant plane roars
Gently as a carrier-pigeon, soon
Drowned in the distance.
What shall we do?
Before the shadows have engrossed the grass
There is a patch of sun to lie upon —
The pale warm thing that summer sheds
When she's ready to be gone.
The peaceful fragrance has not passed
From the fleece that she has worn.
Fear nothing. Hush.
The full bough, the bush, the dreaming vine
Vie with lush greens. To what should sleepy grief
Open its eyes again?
One leaf, blood-bright, stains silence
Like a cry.

To a Friend Who Fears Revolution

The fragile penates are threatened, the porcelain, the blown
Glass, and the box of sweet sounds, and satiny woods,
Lares lovingly wrought, worshiped as gods and goods,
These may be ravished, dismembered, overthrown!
And these gone, what goes too? The hearth is shaken
By no violence native to earth or air,
But by the mob, the arch-Goth, that cannot care
For an image smashed, an idolatrous heart forsaken.
These propped, these sheltered you, powerful though frail
These magnified your house, miraculously
Extended time. Are they endangered? You see
Life shrink, peace fly, animal strength prevail.
Secure them now, who have so well defended
You, saved you: themselves they cannot save.
Seal doors, keep close, nor listen. Without a grave,
Justice lies crying for burial unattended.

Study in Black and White

It was all eminently
appropriate.
The whites were in white,
the blacks were in black,
the clergy was in half-mourning.
The large horse-faced lady
in the picture hat
sat across the aisle
from the rabbit-faced little lady
who was trying to control, vainly,
the shaking of her head.
A dozen
not too pretentiously shabby
painters, poets, musicians
applauded
the well-groomed manored ladies and gentlemen
applauding
the conspicuously neat scions of slaves
singing
'God's Goin' to Set This World on Fire.'

Quiet Places

The pears are yellowing on the branch,
The room composes
Around the mellow stains of lamps;
Though scattered feathers on the wood path mutely
Accuse the bloody beak and claws
Of last night's sleek murderer who spent the day in sleep.
Beauty ripens,
Beauty still reposes, leaning against a bar of orchard light,
Or at night in rooms that answer love
And shelter wit.
There are quiet places.
But of certain things refuse to speak
Even where fruit hangs mild, even where the lamp is lit —
Or, behind the leaves,
You may hear a creature grieving,
From the shadows there may stare
Bludgeoned faces.

Free Lecture

The room is public. But in their ranged places
How separate, how intent upon the flame
Each shelters from his neighbor's breath, these faces,
Set sharply aloof, and curiously the same,
Being wrought to one pitch of thirst, bound to one grief
Over shabbiness striven with, how many years.
Oh, thirst for beauty, making beauty beyond belief,
Where the grace of laughter is lost with the peace of tears!

On the Unemployed

*Being a Timely Rejoinder to Gerard Manley Hopkins'
Sonnet on the Same Theme*

Tom's cold, cold. Shrugs closer to dour Dick
And Harry, sick
Of his empty guts, slack hands that no work fills.
The street's no harsher than these faces, chills
No less than the cold heavens with their trick
Of making spire, dome, breathing breast seem quick
With light that in its jewelling passage spills
Hope, lustre —
And is quenched: rouses and stills
All in a moment,
Leaving eyes dazed, heart sick.
Is this all then — to be empty, sick, cold,
Peace gone, courage worn to thin filth like those rags?
Were you born to this end, men?
Would you die old?
Tom shudders. Dick grudges a curse. Harry gags.
Come away. Here's death. Here's nothing. Here if we see at
    all we see how far we fail,
Prisoned in the world's winter, no will to break jail.

Broadway Nocturne

And in the night the legless men go coasting
On noisy wheels across the paving-stones,
Maneuvering the curbs well. In low tones
Women offer flowers, or chewing-gum; some, boasting
No goods, not even the shabbiest beauty, hold out
A tin cup into which passers-by drop a penny
And sometimes even dimes, but mostly not any
Coin at all: they're in a hurry, it's cold out.
In front of the dance-halls the lights glitter and wink,
But the faces of the doormen are as enormously quiet
As a planned murder. The crowd stares, chatters, churns on.
The legless men glance at the sky and think
Of rain. The taxis will profit by it.
The stars are hidden. The cold arc-light burns on.

The Cheerful Voice

The day unfolding like a newspaper
Presents the weather: cloudy, possible rain,
Or — cold, no change. Presents the breakfaster
With buttered toast, another low in grain,
A rise in steel, the crashing of a plane,
With obits of great men, small deaths by choice,
And smashing of the line. At night he'll hear
The same bad news in the same cheerful voice.

At night he'll crouch, miles from the microphone,
Nursing his glass, tapping his cigarette,
Or trying to let the painful spot alone,
Trying to listen, remember, and forget;
Thinking: the tubes have not been mended yet;
Weighing acceptance, wanting to refuse;
Waiting the brazen advice in the golden tone
Of the same cheerful voice that tells the same bad news.

There are the hours between, of streets and streets,
Brownstone decaying among dingy brick,
Cool neon pulsing red, the stony seats
Along the leafless park, the blind man's stick
Tapping, the bland plate glass, the endless thick
Horned clamor, and, cause at last to rejoice:
The bright cellophane smile declaring it defeats
The same bad news in the same cheerful voice.

There are the hours between and the eleventh hour,
The dark night that no stars, no lamps can light,
No fire can warm, no dynamo empower,
When the soul taking grim measure of its fright
Hears the tread on the stair, the knock at the door, the tight
Grip on the holster, the cough of doom — a ruse —
And yet endures. Endures till doom devour
The cheerful voice that tells the same bad news.

'Peace in Our Time'

Fortressed by bookwalled rooms,
Or at ease, reclined in
Chairs set out under trees in an innocent landscape,
These were the wise, these were the well-defended.
Music
Weaving far legends on a warp of air
Was richly theirs.
The primitive mask amused them.
They were those also
Delighting in the leaf, the evening planet,
The laughter of children, the admired game.
All this is ended.

They have known waiting
In shrouded cities, listened to the bray of
The loud-speaker, and the crowd replying.
They have blinked, under sunlit trees, at the noise of a
Homing plane.
They have looked, one at another, their words quenched,
Their hearts stifled, their eyes alone
Uttering their unease,
In the bookwalled room, with the lights shining.

Debate Between the Mind and Heart
of the Poet

'No time for tears!'
                    'A time to clean the guns?
Yet reading Harry Heine's spotted page,
You must admit a salty fluid runs
When the heart's pricked.'
                          'A song-bird in a cage;
Remember that the sick Jew cooled his rage
With melancholy: whining poetry!'
'A poet's phrase.'
                'And from a century
Shut from all rumors of the wars we wage,
In convent quarrels: Donne, too, was a dunce.'
'A lover.'
            'Living in another age.'

'His songs delight us still, and Keats delights,
Though sighing like a west wind in his odes
And sonnets heavy as the feverish nights
With his heart-crowding sorrow.'
                    'Say he loads
The rifts with ore; not all those glittering nodes
Dazzle us now. Better a base alloy,
Or lead for bullets, than a silver toy;
Go set your jewels in the heads of toads
In fairy tales to please a dreamy boy.
Not flutes, but trumpets!'
                'Barricades, not roads?'

'Go build them.'
           'Barricades?'
                   'And trenches too.
All other roads lead nowhere.'
                  'To the grave.'
'What Milton did, a poet yet may do.'
'Fight?'
        'His pen fought.'
               'I would be brave,
If I could find a paradise to save,
But I am bound and blind; hell holds me here.'
'The time is short.'
          'I know.'
              'Another tear?'
'The time is short.'
           'Fool, use it!'
                 'Call me knave,
Not fool: wisdom is sad, and has known fear,
Riding the flood, whereof our time's a wave.'

The World of Tomorrow

Now, preparing the Fair, they speak of tomorrow.
They cross striped trouser-legs, one lifts his chin
(The iron jaw under the velvet skin)
From a formal collar. The throat as a tower
Of ivory was Solomon's fine thought,
Who dealt in ivory, and in spices and hides,
Gold, silver, pomegranates, and what besides
Could be shipped f.o.b., having been bought
Cheaply, to sell at what the traffic would bear.
They speak of tomorrow, building alabaster
Towers, but in the brief splendor of plaster,
Bold ramps jutting on the empty air.
O gaiety of blue and orange domes!
Miracles of speed and magnitude,
The eyeless windows, the synthetic wood,
The metal easy-chairs, the bright glass homes!
Pennants ballooning, color everywhere,
The booths, the bands, swing-music, souvenirs,
The tricks of chemists and of engineers,
The crowds that taste and try and push and stare,
Grasping at tomorrow, which is not to be seen
Even with television or the electric eye,
Or spun from the smashed atom or announced by the lie-
Detector, or any yet more marvellous machine.
Tomorrow will come, naturally, like death
(Old-fashioned death: we have refused to import
The clever Japanese or the noisy Italian sort).
Oh, it will come more quietly than a bud from its sheath.
It was prepared before and after the Flood,
In Egypt, and in Rome; some think Richelieu

Put a jewelled finger on it, and Metternich too
Would have played obstetrician if he could;
But tomorrow is not in the hands of a man or a nation,
Though it has been shaped by Moscow and Madrid,
And all that we left undone and all that we did,
The late sleep, the paid kiss, the hands in the golden basin.
This is not quite what they mean, these gentlemen
Planning the Fair, eager to promote trade,
Make friends, make money, make what can be made,
Mapping a new world with a streamlined pen.
They are deceived; we know it otherwise,
The familiar features that we cannot place
(O in what mirror have we met that face?)
We know this world, the craters of those eyes.
How shall we bear their look?
                                        How shall we bear
The rowdy jazz, the laughs, the jolly fun,
Or the polite pose of deafness to which we run
From tomorrow's image and tonight's despair?

The impresario is unimpressed,
Delighting in his triangle and sphere,
Blocks of a nursery world he can build here
To cheer the mob who all hope for the best,
And think of the future as something on which to borrow,
Not as the glory for which the world was made.
Nor do we think of it so, who are ashamed and afraid
Now. Preparing the Fair, they speak of tomorrow.

The Remnant

What ails you now
That you are gone up to the housetops
O you that are full of shoutings,
A tumultuous city, a joyous?

They are gone up to the housetops
Windows, balconies crowded
A press of men in the streets
It will be soon now

                   Not Sennacherib heard it

Never was heard in Asia
This thick mob-mouthed thunder
Shouts roars multitudes cheering.
Pours from houses and pavements

                         enormous machinal

Thousand-throated frenzy.
Now
Motors flanked by machine guns
Tear gas bombs held ready
Armored cars bristling

                   Not invincible Caesar

Rode so panoplied. Smiling
Comes, in an armored car, steel vest under trench cloth,
Shouts acclamations rejoicings

                   Comes . . .

Make an uproar, O ye peoples,
And ye shall be broken in pieces,
And give ear, all ye of far countries:

HE comes
Bows from his armored
Car, answers salute with salute

Bows across barrage of
Dark shirts, faces frozen
Above fixed bayonets

                        Make an uproar

(Smiling)

                        All ye of far countries

(Salute)

                        And ye shall be broken in pieces

The housetops lie in the street
The pavements shudder beneath their
Burden   the dead hurled
With the living

                  Broken in pieces
The smoke curls upward

                     broken
What is the noise of a city?
Wheels, horns, radios, voices

                      raised in anger, in laughter,
Murmur of multitudes   muffled mutter of traffic.
What are these noises?
The whine of a shell   the split
Scream   the ambulance sirens,
The groans of a thousand.

                Give ear, all ye of far countries.
The house-walls clutter the street
Grins from an upper storey

                  flesh torn from the bone
The furniture, broken in pieces.
(The movie palace was crowded.)

34

There are the subways for refuge
At the entrance you meet them
Women, big-bellied children, swollen with wind,
Or they wander
                            beyond the city limits
In the corridors of the mines
                                        you will find them asleep
                        The summer fruits are not gathered.

                        Give ear, all ye of far countries.
                        Where they prepare the table,
                        They spread the carpets,
                        They eat, they drink,
Where there are lights and singing
Wine of choice and a swing song
Lights on the burnished hair, flesh luminous as jewels,
Lights in the eyes that glaze
The throat shaken with laughter
                        Your slain are not slain with the sword
                        Neither are they dead in battle.

                        What will you do
                        In the desolation which shall come?
                        To whom will you flee for help?
                        And where will you leave your glory?
                        They shall bow down under the prisoners and
                                shall fall under the slain.

And those in the joyous city?
They shall come down from the housetops

They shall go up from the streets

                       separately and alone

Who shared in the glory

Will look for their portion

                 and find it

To each his mouthful of malice

To each his fistful of hate.

Who heard the shouts behind shutters

Who heard the shouts and were silent

Will take what is given

Some to meet in the camps

                   over the filth of latrines

Some to meet by the wall

                facing the guns

Some to meet in the pit

                 where the suicides are flung

Some never to meet, but to sit

In darkened chambers, alone

The sun hidden from them

The lamp at evening unlit

What passes for thought among them

Revolving with envy

About the fate of an exile

           Watchman, what of the night?

The sun is hidden from us

The light of the moon is dimmed

But the pharos shines

            At the airport

The word is

                    ceiling unlimited
A clear night for bombing
And after

The cave, the abandoned mine
                              the subway crowded with sleepers
Darkness over the city
Darkness over the village
And over the pastures, darkness
Over the orchards and fields
Darkness over the vineyards.
                    Watchman, what of the night?
How does it pass in the trenches?
In the hospital and the prison?
What of the night of exile?

And those not slain with the sword,
Nor with the gun and the
Bayonet.
Those dead,
But not dead in battle.
The dead who are poisoned with power
The dead in the places of power
Who are buying and selling the nations
Dealers in houses and land and works and bread and munitions
Those dead, but not dead in battle
The dead who own the living.
                    To whom will they flee for help?
                    And where will they leave their glory?
The people are starving

The people are fed on lies
There is death in the pot
The poor are devoured by lack
                    the coffin is bought on credit
The rich are asking
                    Which mountains are free for skiing?
For sunning, what southern beaches?
The passports are ready, crisply
The letters of credit folded.
Billions for battleships
                    the contracts are quickly prepared
How much to rebuild
                    the laboratory in ruins?
O Attila! O Alexander!
The delightful city
                    is become a madhouse
The populous earth
                    is become a cemetery
Sargon also
Governed by thuggery
The dead against the living.

But the remnant
Who lie out in the fields
Or watch in the cities,
                    or wait
In the prisons,
                    or work
Where the oppressor is strong.
Those who refuse madness

Those who resist death
Those whose mouths are not stopped
By the guns
                    or the wails of the children
Whose hearts are not to be broken
Whose minds are not to be broken
Whose will is not to be broken

Go up to the housetop, Watchman
                                        What of the night?

A Contemporary's Hymn to Isis

Dispersed and spent,
As in legend the limbs of Osiris
Crying one to another, the unknowing undying
Scattered limbs of the god:
On the winter waters
Lie
The hand without fingers,
The feet without speed,
The head without thought, the torse hacked and adrift
And its heart in a house without windows
Beaten upon by the sea:
Unknowing undying.

Where were you then, my sister, my soul?
Seeking
Through the two kingdoms, imploring
The Upper Region, the Lower, getting no answer?
Asking the birds of the sky
Who deceived you and vanished?
We called you,
We the sad limbs in dispersion.

In vain.

But flying you sought us.
The dead could not stop you.
No, nor the horns of Evil
Those that undid us.
And we cried, scattered.
Cried, and were mute.

And you came, O soul, my sister,
Flying, quick with compassion, the sleepless mother,
Unwearied bride.
Restored
To the hand its fingers, and speed to the feet,
And the heart
Beating again in the body, healed and made whole,
And the brow
Crowned with thought, lord of the nether kingdom.

Now, united,
Shall we not rule?
Can we forgive and govern?
You beside me, and I
That lately was many, scattered and tossing
On the horns of the
Savage dividing waters,
Can we endure?
Death under our sceptre. O
Sharper than death, unpersuadable Evil
Behind and before us?

Do not
Speak, mother and bride, my sister:
We that were
Scattered, now are made one,
We that were
Parted, now are at peace.
O do not
Lay a lightest feather upon the scales
Held in equipoise of triumphant silence.

Now, my sister, my soul, serenely remember
As I serenely foresee
The workings of Evil, past and to come.
Nor deny —
Denial only is dying —
This moment of union.

II

Wine Party

As coins because they shine
Remain unspent,
The golden-bodied wine
Will first content
The pure lust of the eye.
Enough, if such rich lustre pay the sight
With interest upon long vanished light.

This pleasure as it pales
Seems not so fine
As what the glass exhales:
Breath of the vine.
Rare gust, be slow to die!
We'll take it on the tongue, mixed with our breath
The ghostly grape laughs jollily at death.

The wine, though cool as snow,
Being drunk, is fire.
The taste transmutes the glow,
Until desire
Puts its long grieving by,
Or finds some savor of sweetness in what's tart.
Though wrung, the heart exults, the shuddering heart.

The failure of delight
That makes us rage,
The treachery, the spite
Of this fouled age,
Wine's power can defy.
The blood bounds in the vein, flesh unsubdued
Forgets its pain, the soul forgets its solitude.

Record by Yvette Guilbert

On the wall
Jane Avril
Flaunts violent stripes,
Bends her head
Too boldly for a dancer dead.
C'EST le mai!
Below, the slow revolving disc
Quickening gives out
A shout
That recalls
The bones, the jowl, the black gloves, the yellow gown
Set down with Toulouse-Lautrec's
Savage stroke.
C'est le MAI!
Who was it sang?
Who was it spoke?
Dancer, painter, old diseuse,
Anarchists and Fascists must
Come to dust.
But the rich
Malice, the gay lust refute
The tomb, the war, and the listeners, smiling silently
In the polite room.
C'EST LE JOLI MOIS DE MAI!

New York * December * 1931

The child's cough scratches at my heart — my head
Buzzes with rumors of war, appalling news
From China, and queer stories of men bred
In ant-hills which will overthrow the world.
Machines can split the atom, if you choose,
And hens turn into cocks, I have heard said.
This does not unsteady my pulses.
Thoughts arc hurled
East, west, and up and down the universe,
But none so dizzying as the sitting still,
In lamplight, among friends
(The cough's not worse?)
And watching eyes beam, lips move, fingers drill
Gently upon the table . . .
Oh, clever, oh, kind!
Here time undoes itself, here we rehearse
A drama not debated by the mind,
And see in fair beginnings fairer ends.
Say children cry, with reason, and men die,
Unreasonably, say our hearts are torn
And our brains puzzled — miracles persist!
Not the halved atom nor the changeling bird,
But this, the dazzling moment, close and human,
That for long pain makes brief complete amends.

Memory of a Journey

Not for gardens, not for thick-leaved slopes
Heavy with green dark silences:
Not for the road the wheels unwind
Smoothly from giant spools, ahead
And under,
Broad, blind, leaving
The gardens and the streets, the shops, fields, hills behind:
Not for this
The restless eye asks vainly
And again.
But for that land .
No cedar shadows, where no lemon shines,
Where no corn springs, no vine,
No flower, no bird.

Bare,
Or sown
By the wind only
With writhen weed,
Grown as from ocean seed.
Sand.
There is a salty landscape
Eyes constrained
To try through tears —
The tongue has tasted them —
Approve:
The wind-shaped moor, sea-bred, not more unkind
Than human love.

Truro Hour

Carved by the silence, clean as rock
The moors lie open to the sky.
Each bearded dune stands like a stock
In early nudity.
No shadow stirs, to crack the spell
Cast by the heat upon this waste
That shows the candor of a shell
To heavens as bare, as chaste.
Alone coarse beach-grass, shaggy pine
Find sea-grudged root beneath the sand,
And stubborn as the wind, define
The salt lagoon from the salt land.
White as the surf, white as the sun,
The cottages cling sleepily
Each to its hillock, one and one,
Like sea-fed gulls beside the sea.
Between its knees this naked place
Holds the strange peace that is secured
To those who smile in their embrace
At violence dreaded or endured.

Insufficiency

What though the moon pours restlessness?
The stars in unison are uttering peace.
The trees are shapes of stillness that no wind
Nor sudden bird can stir from their dark trance.
If there's a soul whose stature is no less
Than the huge night, it need ask no release.
But one that's ragged, one that's lame and blind,
Shudders to hear the silent heavens dance.

Brief Solace

Some turn to wild shreds in the western sky
Hanging, torn, on pent-houses and spires,
Stained saffron veils shed over roofs and wires —
Some choose such rags of heaven, and think to lie
Softly, at last, staunching the pain with these.
Some grip the strength of hills, some cool their fever
In a known stream, for the inconstancy
Of water is apparent only : see,
How steadfast as a mountain is a river!
From these old roots mortality sucks ease.
Yet there are those whom the continuous show
Of earth, those whom the streamers of
The bannered ether touch as with a glove,
And who salute these things and let them go,
Indifferent to their cold courtesies.
Men of this temper find no comfort else
But such as lives in face and voice, or stammers
With the stammering heart, or sparkles when mind hammers
On forging mind. Alone what's human spells
Brief solace for immortal cruelties.

Gasoline Letter
(*After a motor-trip*)

Not men had built this road, not men had planted
These orchards, cleared these fields; we felt, unseen,
A Gargantuan hand unroll the ribbon
Under us, enchanting the machine;
A Hand removing time with our smooth motion,
Enchanting us to forgive the cruel year.
Such happiness is supernatural — name it,
It crumbles, and is fear.
We were half afraid, watching the yellow willows
Beside their silver sons; the blue increase
Of sky, leaving the clouds behind; the tawny
Autumn touch in the ash trees; the sunned fleece
Of upland pastures; drinking the wind; meeting
The lakes' dark gentle eyes.

                              And we were mute,
Crying, Remember — thinking of famine: Remember
The true taste of this fruit.

Autumn Moment

Neither small scudding birds
Nor dragonflies,
But high notes scattered in descending
Scales upon the page:
These leaves.
Sky's marginal
To the clear imprint floated on the gale.
Their music
Sparkles in mid air, lending
The eyes another sense.
In golden blankness
Transience folds her wings,
To hear the song
That siren silence sings.

Sub Specie Aeternitatis

No music can contain this
Hour snatched out of time, when to look up
To the clear arc
Is bodilessly to climb
The ridge-pole of heaven, swing through the blue tent,
So, burning with tall cold,
Exceed the bliss
Of marrying sound with sound.
Nor any wind
Stains the pure hush, breathes on
The brimming peace.
But to perfect
Silence —
Single, gold, one leaf
Swerves to the ground,
And being gone,
A crane
Like a slow arrow through the empty air
Moves truly,
Never to be seen again.

Elegy on the Death of W.B.Yeats

'Words alone are certain good':
But we cannot speak or sing
Now that mouth is dumb.
No more will the lion come
Raging from the wood's dark heart,
Though the world is torn apart
For his ravening.
The wild swan that rode the flood
In pride has taken wing.

Vain words, they cannot summon up
The lion that he was, the swan
That so took our eyes.
The stern figure will not rise,
Nor stir our age's sweetest tongue.
The song, the laugh that mocked the song,
Both are air, are gone.
He has left us all to sup
With Dante and with Donne.

Not words, but howling winds that call
His rock-borne images to mind,
Fit him at the close.
He does not require the rose
That to its rich core he knew.
Wintry music is his due
Of a noble kind.
Sound, then, for his funeral
The sea's note on the wind.

Savage indignation tore
That laboring breast too long,
Yet his laughter rang,
Yet the marching-tune he sang
Shakes the roads. Will stiff lips utter
Nothing? Neither eyelid flutter
When a jest is flung?
Cliffs those echoes leap no more
Give back, repeat his song.
What words, when swanless waters beat the shore?

After Music

These eyes are strangely learned
In imaging each thing
Grown to the fabulous:
The sombre cloud as the burned
Arabian wonder's pyre;
The pale spoil of the beach
As petal-drift of stone;
Winged serpents in the fire.
But the quick eyes must fail
When music moves to fill
The reaches of the mind —
Their skill is of no avail.
For what image can contain
The grieving of the strings,
The trumpets' triumph and threat?
Thought must fall back again
Before the majesty
And sweetness of those sounds
Whose superhuman joy
Is darkness to the eye.
Oh, on what do you brood,
Heart blind with ecstasy,
When the low flutes call you
Home to beatitude?

Solstice

Here in the lap of summer, in the silence
Sharpening every voice:
The bird's,
The boy's spiralling laughter,
Stillness folds
Itself upon itself, like the blunt hills.
And grows,
No more mysterious than a flower states
Its color to the sun.
Here's a boy's joy
In the arrow that finds its mark,
But man learns
Houndlike devotion to a universe
Whose evil is not measured, and whose careless
Unhoped-for love
Only dark patience earns.

Child

This flesh, ignorant of itself,
Bodies the light of morning it may not seize,
Bodies the unearthly, the impalpable gold
Sifted through glass, fallen about its knees.

It is a creature wavering and intent,
Being so often assaulted, every sense
Assailed — a tender animal wrestling
Ambiguously with omnipotence.

It utters snub syllables, sings, even,
In such a voice as might be wrung
From a bird on an Arabian tree
Or cherubim's incredible lung.

Muscled with quicksilver, its motion
Is of impetuous water under wind:
Soft, stubborn, innocent, abrupt to turn and
Leave a wreck behind.

Grosser than flame or flower, it is in nature
Flowerlike, in essence, flame. It will have fled
When it has first found its yesterdays.
And how, then, shall the heart be comforted?

A Birthday Song for Alison (Alisoun)

From ear to heart rejoicings run
To hear the news of Alison.
Forever sweet be the renown —
Or old or young — of Alisoun!
The merriest bells chime in her name,
By any spelling 'tis the same:
A sound, a round, a carol of fun
Lapped in the syllables: Alisoun;
A boon, a tune, a rune to crown
Magic with melody: Alison.
Her mother's name is wisdom's own,
Her dad's means iron's way with stone;
Thus light and power have joined as one
To make most excellent Alison.
And let us tell her brother's fame
Which adds fair stature to her name,
And all proclaim in unison
Our blessings upon Alisoun!

Zoo

Ape

His eyes are mournful, but the long lined palm
He thrusts between the bars expects the best.
His old man's face as innocent as calm,
The beggar puts compassion to the test
And fails. He grips the bars; his pained stare grows
To a brown study framed in dusty fur.
He has a cold. He sneezes, cleans his nose,
Then gravely licks a flexile forefinger.
A pause; the bald mauve hand from which men shrink,
The fingers, strong to clutch, quick to explore,
Again extended, are again refused.
The eyes, poor sorrow's jewels, seldom wink,
But to his grinning public, as before,
Show endless patience, endlessly abused.

Young Gazelle

Stiff as her Egyptian counterpart
She stays, on legs of matchstick ivory,
Rigid to hide the racing of her heart,
Though the black boss of her enormous eye
Flames inconsolable. Less like a deer
Than like a freckled girl, her skin's blanched gold
Drawn over little bones, her head held clear,
She listens, as if breathing were too bold.
A tremor, and she is still. Now sunny peace,
Light as the straw beneath her feet, persuades
Her pulses briefly, till the terror goes.
Whipped by a childish whimsy of release,
She caracoles: a quick bound that evades
The bars. Then drops into a thrilled repose.

Rhinoceros

Formed with the mountains in the Miocene,
Dull sire to the skittish unicorn
A virgin tames, how heavily serene
He stands, this noontime, tendering his horn
To the soiled keeper's boot-sole. Neither knows
That the rude object offered for caress
Was hunted, like the Grail or like the Rose,
And, crushed, once medicined His Holiness.
The monster moves his head, he does not move
His piggish eyes, his body in its plates
Of leathern armature, stuffed well with grass.
Night was made for wandering and for love,
The day for sleeping: but not here. The gates
Close. The keeper goes. Hours, like ages, pass.

Zebra Finch

Tearing the lettuce — hard vermilion,
This tiny beak that fills this tiny crop
Slid earthward at a pricking of the sun:
A clot of color in a pointed drop.
About the throat — an inch of evening
When green and turquoise struggle in surrender,
The little scrap of scarf's a bluer thing
Than heaven's silken azure, and more tender.
But the bird's prison-tagged, his tail-tip barred
Like jungle shade in stripes of black and white,
His radiance pieced out with mourning wear.
Taking that badge of sorrow as his guard,
He shreds his lettuce-leaf in shy delight,
And dares to glow a moment on the air.

Lioness Asleep

Content that now the bleeding bone be swept
Out of her reach, she lay upon her side.
In a blonde void sunk deep, at last she slept,
Bland as a child and breathing like a bride.
Color of noons that shimmer as they sing
Above the dunes, her sandy flanks heaved slow.
Between her paws curled inward, billowing
Waves of desert silence seemed to flow.
The crowd was gone, the bars were gone, the cage
Thinned into air, the sawdust and the fleas
Winnowed by sleep to nothing. After food,
Absence possessed her: bliss keener than rage,
If slumber's prisoner at a bound could seize
This ghostly freedom, lapping it like blood.

Sea Lion

Sleeker than water, solid as that rock
Where, grappling amorous jaws, the others play,
He curves upon himself, from the wet flock
Apart. This lion has the serpent's way
Of coiling into a cold monument
To secrecy. His dun thick massive shape
Poured, nape to tail, in slumber's mold, he went
Toward self-exile as toward escape.
His fingered flippers trail upon the sand.
His streamlined head slopes backward on his own
Smooth shoulder. On his lip, humorously,
Antennae-like the separate whiskers stand:
These live. He, sealed in solitude like stone,
Is frozen stiff as his own solemn sea.

Black Panther

This little panther wears a coat of soot,
Well-suited so. Stretched out along his shelf,
Still, if not brooding storm, the sultry brute
Looks soft as darkness folded on itself.
His limbs, his tarry torso, are as mat
As night wanting the stars; their resting grace
Lies leashed. Alone his head's erect: pure cat
Stares, alive with danger, in that face.
From the sharp ears down to the finest hair
At his tail's tip, he might be carved of coal.
Child of the shadows, he appears as tame,
Till, from behind the grate, the gold eyes glare
With such a light as could consume the whole
To ashes and a memory of flame.

III

Problem

Strange heart, that knows not whether it loves or no,
Or, loving, loves a stranger or a friend!
Here is a puzzle without beginning or end,
Subtle as Chinese ivories. Oh, slow
And baffled heart, how many hours, weeks, years,
Will you be returning to this, abandoning it,
And again returning? The design's exquisite,
And torment has enchantments, it appears.

Is it only a game? A thing to make time move
When twilight crowds the room, and the wind blows east?
The hero's heart is his solitary feast,
But bitterer is this employ of love.
And would one solve the problem, daring to send
Its pieces to the unknown, to the beloved?
What then were proved thereby, and what disproved?
Do not entreat the stranger, heart, do not question the friend!

Then and Now

Even love-in-a-fog, love-in-a-cloud,
Is pain, but worse the pang of times remembered,
When the streets, the river, were bannered
With heaven, and the heart proud —
The heart that now like a trapped animal
Pants, rends, and cries aloud.
Were those years good? They were hardly to be borne.
Youth that was cloudy, foggy, clogged with grief.
Yet memory goes back, compassionate memory,
Who best knows how to forget, binds up the torn
And ragged places, washes every stain,
Cries: heart, you were happy, could you change this grief
For that old pain.
So love that is not love returns to repair
The loss of youth with strange regret for joy
That was not joy, and therewith grief grows bold.
The river, the streets, are changed,
The heavens above me are different, and the boy
Beside me will not know till he is old
How time, curing the heart, can bring it to despair.

Pause

Before the night comes, before the day goes,
In the hesitant hour,
In the season of hesitation, a wind blows
Honey of youth remembered, like a flower
Invisible, to shake the heart's repose.

Before day goes, before night comes, when the reins
Of thought hang slack,
The mind puts by its journey and its pains,
But the troubled heart looks forward, again looks back,
The wine of heaven so charging through the veins.

Before the day ebbs, before the night flows,
In a pause
Strange as the light that narrows toward its close,
Music, against the stern voice of the laws,
Cries out with chilling sweetness once, and goes.

Two People Eat Honey

Beyond the window the moon may be in riot
with the winter night. But your voice having ceased
in the room here, silence comes, naked-footed,
to cover the leavings of our frugal feast.
Your hands lie on the table, clasped, quiet.
Kind as an old servant, silence moves
about us, with a tender dignity smoothing
the unseemly creases in our loves
Your eyes upon me stir no more than the rooted
shadow beside your chair. Your eyes know
upon what song silence has locked her throat.
The melody trembles toward us, still too low
to name, though the music mounts above our breathing,
mounts, and mingles with, far off, a train
that pants harshly of journeys. Your eyes upon me.
We are alone again.

At the Battery

Over the waters, polished
Pitch-bright in the darkness,
The funnel dipping, the lantern
Swinging: yellow, a stripe
Falling across the cabin's
Cosy shabbiness, cutting
Out of the shadows a worn
Face, and a blackened pipe.

Soft incessant insistent
Puffs of steam in the offing.
Close, on the quay, a sailor
Turns an indifferent stare
From his business of pumping;
Water flushes the planks, and
Ceasing, silence swallows
The simple scene like air.

No more. This was sufficient
To make fabulous midnight
Earnest, real and lonely.
River and lantern webbed
The men, the tug, the moorage
In a steady fluxion,
As the heart swelled slowly
And the swift hour ebbed.

Midsummer Night

Midnight, and a tigerish sky
In whose wild wide lovely flank
Throbbed one planet and the moon:
Two golden holes, two wounds gone dry.
Not of these would the night die
That ranged so beautiful and rank
Above us. Yet it must die soon.

Gone, it cannot shine again.
The dark bright fleece will heave no more,
Scattered, beyond human chart.
Nor ragged stripe nor spark remain
Of all that glory and that pain.
Can a dead night find claws to score
The living heart?

Frustrate

As when a car stalls where the traffic's thickest,
So, while passing hours speed friend and stranger
To meet the pleasure promised or the danger
Sought, and horns hound most where lights are quickest,
I am caught, and cannot back or go.
An engine with too heavy a load to bear
Balks, though policeman signals, the chauffeur
Rages, and it is late, the street clocks show.
I am the hot chauffeur, the car, the traffic cop,
The passenger, resigned — I am them all.
Here is no reason to despair, we'll move,
If to some unguessed place, before we stop;
Perhaps, like old Aeneas, yet recall
This halt, smiling. Heart, what will that smile prove?

The Dispassionate Shepherdess

Do not live with me, do not be my love.
And yet I think we may some pleasures prove
That who enjoy each other, in the haste
Of their most inward kissing seldom taste.

Being absent from me, you shall still delay
To come to me, and if another day,
No matter, so your greeting burn as though
The words had all the while been packed in snow.

No other gift you'll offer me but such
As I can neither wear, nor smell, nor touch —
No flowers breathing of evening, and no stones
Whose chilly fire outlasts our skeletons.

You'll give me once a thought that stings, and once
A look to make my blood doubt that it runs,
You'll give me rough and sharp perplexities,
And never, never will you give me ease.

For one another's blessing not designed,
Marked for possession only of the mind,
And soon, because such cherishing is brief,
To ask whereon was founded the belief

That there was anything at all uncommon
In what each felt for each as man and woman —
If this then be our case, if this our story,
Shall we rail at heaven? Shall we, at worst, be sorry?

Heaven's too deaf, we should grow hoarse with railing.
And sorrow never quickened what was failing.
But if you think we thus may pleasures prove,
Do not live with me, do not be my love.

Hard Case

She moves from rage to woe,
From ice to fever.
The touch that would relieve her
She will not ever know,
And sleep is slow.

Which ague is the worse,
The rage — the sorrow?
Today her rage, tomorrow
Her sorrow is the curse
That she must nurse.

Though getting no relief,
She has assurance
That what is past endurance
Must pass, and so be brief.
This swells her grief!

Intimate View

This is the private face, stupid as crime,
The hair, the mouth awry, eyes thick with tears:
The image of the stained disordered years
Marked by the vengeance of insulted time.
Weakness is cruel, violent and crass,
Yet cannot kill the thing on which it stares,
That feeble self for which alone it cares
Mirrored as in unshatterable glass.
It cannot run, it cannot even move,
Except toward death or madness, to escape.
It cannot be divorced from its own shape
By any skill, lacking that one of love.
But it can find a moment's bitter ease
In drawing truly what it hates and sees.

Despair Rejoices

Oh, bitter-hearted me, thrice-parted me,
What Pythagorean discipline will wring
From discord, harmony?
And where, out of this quarreling breast,
Shall peace be found?
Since not the earth, the bloody-syllabled,
Not the distracted air,
Affords a ground
For music to build house.
Selves, you are blackguards who inhabit me
As vagabonds do ditches, prisoners: jails —
Bound, being at rest,
And muddied, being free.
Yet now, and though with harsh cracked voices, sing,
Together sing,
And briefly, though joy fails,
Despair rejoices.

The Happy Isles

They say that love, too, has its Fortunate Islands,
Not fabled, not fit for the dead;
But likely out of westering waters lifting
Their drenched-with-sunset head;
Or pale, it may be, as the star of morning,
Or meagre, even, as islands in a lake
That you may see a tethered rowboat nuzzle.
But what airs, oh, of enchantment overtake
Those who set foot upon the incredible beaches!
What winds, what wings, hover, and at their feet
What flowers, or shells, to gather, and on their lips
Blow salty gusts, then sweet.
Some, they say, do know those Fortunate Islands.
Is it only the young? Who on a day must turn
To this harsh country we inhabit,
And cannot leave, or spurn.

What Do We Need?

What do we need for love — a midnight fire
That flings itself by handfuls up the chimney
In soft bright snatches? Do we need the snow,
Gentle as silence, covering the scars
Of weeks of hunger, years of shabbiness?
Summer or winter? A heaven of stars? A room?
The smiling mouth, the sadness of desire,
Are everywhere the same. Let lovers go
Along an unknown road: they will find no less
What is familiar. Let them stay at home,
And all will still be strange. This they best know,
Who with each heartbeat fight the fear of change.

Memory Poised

As on the throat of some museum piece,
On this chaste air is inlay of gold leaf
Quieter there
Than sun on cheek, abstract as emperor's jewel
Cased in glass, truer than enamel.
Tumult of swollen waters on the rocks
Below, remote as rare,
Exalts the sovereign silence.
Balancing
Stiff leaf and stubborn wave,
The tug chugging, the enormous
Strain of the delicate piers, the cloud, the light,
And cinders on the track behind,
The hour
Is silverly suspended.
Insecure, lay this upon some high shelf of the mind,
Not for the eyes
But for the heart to come
Back to, reclaim, and, more than art, admire:
Memory poised
Briefly in tragic equilibrium.

Dogma

Love is not true: mathematicians know
Truth, that's alive in heaven, and in the mind —
Out of our bodies; you will never find
Love strict as number, and enduring so.
It is not free: alone the grave's narrower
Than the little space in which this passion moves,
With a door that opens inward: he who loves
Measures his paces like a prisoner.
They who give it large names are liars, or
They are fools. More softly, you and I,
Slow to assert what we can never prove,
Wonder what algebraist, what dictator
Can teach us much of truth or tyranny.
Look at me. Do not speak. But this is love.